The IIA Research Foundation Handbook Series

AUDITING HUMAN RESOURCES

By
Kelli W. Vito, SPHR, CCP

Understanding, Guiding, Shaping

Disclosure

Copyright © 2007 by The Institute of Internal Auditors Research Foundation (IIARF), 247 Maitland Avenue, Altamonte Springs, Florida 32701-4201. All rights reserved. Printed in the United States of America. No part of this publication may be reproduced, stored in a retrieval system, or transmitted in any form by any means — electronic, mechanical, photocopying, recording, or otherwise — without prior written permission of the publisher.

The IIARF publishes this document for informational and educational purposes. This document is intended to provide information, but is not a substitute for legal or accounting advice. The IIARF does not provide such advice and makes no warranty as to any legal or accounting results through its publication of this document. When legal or accounting issues arise, professional assistance should be sought and retained.

The International Professional Practices Framework for Internal Auditing (IPPF) comprises the full range of existing and developing practice guidance for the profession. The IIA's IPPF provides guidance to internal auditors globally and paves the way to world-class internal auditing.

The mission of The IIA Research Foundation (IIARF) is to be the global leader in sponsoring, disseminating, and promoting research and knowledge resources to enhance the development and effectiveness of the internal auditing profession.

ISBN 978-0-89413-614-6
07827 10/07
First Printing

CONTENTS

About the Author v
Acknowledgments vii

PART ONE: Introduction to HR Auditing 1

PART TWO: HR Department Basics 5
   Chapter 1: Strategic Management 9
   Chapter 2: Department Structure and
       Staff Competencies 13
   Chapter 3: HR Facilities 17
   Chapter 4: HR Technology and Information Control 19

PART THREE: Key HR Risk Areas 21
   Chapter 5: Workforce Planning and Employment 23
   Chapter 6: Human Resources Development 33
   Chapter 7: Total Rewards 43
   Chapter 8: Employee and Labor Relations 51
   Chapter 9: Risk Management 57

**PART FOUR: HR Services Outsourcing
and Co-sourcing** 59

APPENDICES
   Appendix A: HR Metrics 63
   Appendix B: Legally Required Notices 67
   Appendix C: Key Employment Regulations 73
   Appendix D: Employment Record Retention 81
   Appendix E: HR Web Sites 83
   Appendix F: Sample Audit Program 87
   Appendix G: References 123

ABOUT THE AUTHOR

Kelli W. Vito, SPHR, CCP, currently is principal of KV Consulting, based in Austin, Texas, which offers strategic human resource management consulting and auditing services to both private and public sector organizations. Her practice specializes in HR auditing, workforce planning, performance management and measurement, strategic planning, compensation administration, and organizational design. Ms. Vito also teaches a variety of management courses. KV Consulting is a certified Texas Historically Underutilized Business.

Prior to starting her own business, Ms. Vito served as the top HR executive for the State of Texas. Her responsibilities included advising over 200 agencies and higher education institutions on all aspects of human resource management. She also testified before the Texas State Legislature and worked extensively on developing workforce regulations. Prior to that role, she served as an audit manager for the Texas State Auditor's Office. She was responsible for performance-related audits and developed the first human resource audit program for the state.

Ms. Vito has her BBA in management and marketing from the University of Texas at Austin. She is a Senior Professional in Human Resources (SPHR) and a Certified Compensation Professional (CCP). She is a member of the Society of Human Resource Management. She was a finalist for the Texas Executive Woman of the Year. Ms. Vito can be reached at kelli.vito@kvconsulting.net.

ACKNOWLEDGMENTS

This Handbook would not have been possible without the support and guidance of The Institute of Internal Auditors' staff and committee members.

I am grateful to my colleague, Mr. LaDair Wright, for his editorial review and comments.

Most importantly, I would like to thank my husband, Frank, for supporting me in all aspects of my life. My daughters, Alyssa and Adrienne, are a constant source of joy and inspiration to me. I would also like to thank my mother, Linda Johns, for her belief that I could do whatever I set out to do.

PART ONE
INTRODUCTION TO HR AUDITING

Human resource management (HR) covers a broad spectrum of workforce activities. Despite its integral role, HR is often considered a "soft" area and management may not understand the inherent risks involved with this function, including employment law issues, compensation and benefit plan design, recordkeeping, and potential fraud issues.

An organization should audit the HR function for these reasons:

- Routine checkup (uncover any unfavorable conditions and set up a treatment plan)
- Determine how to best align HR operations with organizational goals
- Ensure compliance with federal and state employment regulations

To determine what type of audit would be most appropriate for an organization, auditors must examine the current business risks. There are several types of HR audits and all of them focus on different processes or outcomes as outlined below.

Compliance — Risk-based with a focus on legally required aspects of HR such as Family Medical Leave Act, at-will employment, immigration, Fair Credit Reporting Act, discrimination, harassment, COBRA, HIPAA, etc.

Best Practices — Focuses on court decisions that are being used to determine law or administrative systems that reduce errors and omissions, such as hiring and termination processes, performance evaluation processes, disciplinary process and documentation, and litigation or investigation issues.

Strategic — Focuses on systems and processes to determine if they are in line with the strategic plan and whether or not they are helping, hindering, or having little impact. Areas audited might include organizational effectiveness as measured by turnover, length of time to fill an open position, number of employee complaints, and number and cost of unemployment claims lost. It can also uncover ineffective pay practices, pending litigation risks, ineffective training programs, ineffective hiring processes, and poorly designed or administered benefit programs.

Function Specific — Focuses in on a particular area of HR such as compensation, immigration, affirmative action, payroll, benefits, etc."[1]

Scoping an HR audit depends on the organization's budget, risk factors, and available time frame. Oftentimes, it is not practical to conduct a comprehensive audit of the entire HR function. Typically retirement plans, health insurance plans, and deferred compensation programs are considered "out of scope" for an HR audit. Under ERISA, federal law requires employee benefit plans with 100 or more participants to have an audit as part of their obligation to file Form 5500. These audits are conducted on the third-party plan administrators and consist of highly specialized knowledge and procedures. Therefore, these audits are generally conducted by independent CPA firms in order to obtain the audit opinions that are necessary to meet this audit requirement.

Auditors may first focus on the compliance aspect of HR since federal employment regulations are extensive and require organizational diligence to ensure compliance. However, there is also a vital strategic component of HR. The Society for Human

Resource Management defines strategic HR management as the "process of taking a long-term approach to human resource management through the development and implementation of HR programs that address and solve business problems and directly contribute to major long-term business objectives."[2]

In today's environment, some new issues have moved to the forefront in HR, including:

- Executive management ethics.
- Skyrocketing healthcare costs.
- HR outsourcing.
- Baby boomer exodus — labor shortage, aging and diverse workforce.
- Knowledge work — managing knowledge workers.

During a comprehensive HR audit, evidence of these emerging issues may arise.

In a report, findings and recommendations are generally prioritized based upon the risk level assigned to each item. These risk levels include:

High — Legal requirements based upon employment legislation, case law, and compliance. These are items that require immediate attention.

Medium — Best practices that help an organization avoid risks and are, therefore, highly recommended. These are items that should be dealt with in a relatively short time frame as they can easily become high risks if items fall between the cracks.

Low — HR administration best practices. These are administrative suggestions to make the department more effective and efficient."[3]

PART TWO
HR DEPARTMENT BASICS

Auditors should do their homework to understand the basics of the HR function. This will help you to have greater credibility and rapport with HR professionals and make you more efficient during the audit.

If you are planning on conducting a comprehensive review of the HR function, it is important to gain an understanding of how the different HR systems work. Prior to starting the audit, you should consider the following:

- Obtain and review the organization's strategic plan to develop understanding of future workforce needs.

- Obtain and thoroughly review HR strategic and operational plans.

- Review the overall organizational chart to determine the HR department's relationship within the overall structure. Obtain the HR department's organizational chart to better understand function assignments.

- Review employee attitude survey and HR customer survey and any follow-up plans in response to the feedback received.

- Review any performance assessment reports that are specific to the HR department's performance.

- Obtain and review any workforce plans, including recruitment and hiring goals, policies, and procedures.

- Obtain and review any employee turnover statistical reports and employee exit survey results.

- Review employee training plans and course schedules. Specifically request information on supervisory training and new employee orientation.

- Request compensation and benefit policies and procedures documents.

- Request FLSA status listing by job title for all employees.

- Obtain copy of Employee Handbook to identify any oversights or regulation noncompliance.

- Request EEO reports to determine organizational diversity position.

- Obtain a copy of all performance form(s) and request samples of completed evaluations.

- Acquire any relevant reference materials on human resource management.

- Review any recent audit or other assessment reports relating to the HR, training, or payroll functions.

- Survey (by e-mail) managers that are primary customers of HR services.

- Consider interviewing key staff (executive management, CFO, IT director, general counsel, and key management personnel) to get their perspective on the HR function and the service it provides.

- Observe the HR department for a while to see how staff interacts with managers and employees and how work flows.

- Consider performing or purchasing benchmarking/leading practices research/analysis with like entities/industries for comparison to validate the maturity/quality of the HR function.

All of these documents provide critical information that can be used to develop an initial risk assessment and should be discussed in your initial interview with key HR staff. Prepare for your interviews by making a list of questions to direct your thoughts. Talk with the highest-level HR executive to get an understanding of their role and responsibilities. They should be able to give you their perspective regarding concerns they have with current HR systems.

CHAPTER 1
STRATEGIC MANAGEMENT

Restructuring the HR function from an administrative function into a strategic business partner has been a major initiative for many HR professionals in recent years. Auditors may find HR is in some phase of this transition during the audit. Expectations regarding HR's role have changed significantly over time. If HR is functioning at this strategic partner level, then an important partnership of key administrative advisors is formed:

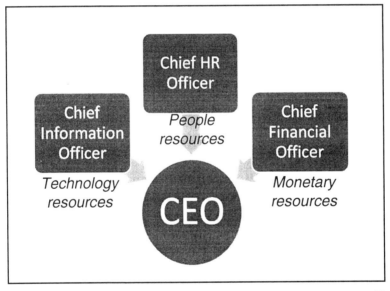

An HR function that has moved into a strategic partner role will exhibit most of the following criteria:

- An HR leader who has a strong knowledge of HR roles and functions, business strategy and operations, and is perceived

as a credible advisor by his/her peers and executive management.
- Top HR position is organizationally on the same level as other program directors and administrative directors (i.e., chief financial officer and chief technology officer).
- HR department is viewed as approachable and trusted to provide accurate information.
- HR department is part of a network of HR departments in peer organizations that share experiences, strategize regarding common problems, and stay abreast of latest HR trends and developments.
- Strategic HR plan is closely linked to the overall business plan.
- Performance assessment of HR programs, including key metrics, is routinely completed.

HR plays a key role in developing systems and programs that support the organization's mission. A detailed examination of the workforce culture, behaviors, and staff competencies promotes the successful execution of business strategy.[4]

Assessing HR's performance is critical for many reasons. It allows management to determine if HR staff is performing at acceptable levels, it helps to determine future strategies, and sometimes it serves as a basis for compensation decisions for staff. Metrics are useful factors that can be measured and tracked to show how HR contributes to the business. (See **Appendix A** for a list of HR metrics.)

Most organizations have a system in place for developing an operating budget. The HR budget should align with the organization's strategic and operational goals. A well-planned and well-documented HR budget demonstrates thoughtful consideration of spending directly linked to the organization's programs and activities.[5]

The data needed to create a new budget include:

- Number of current and projected employees.
- Increased payroll costs due to additional employees, reallocations of selected job classes to higher pay grades, and increases in employee salaries.
- Organizational training and development costs.
- Recruiting costs.
- Cost increases or projected increases to existing benefit programs.
- Current and projected turnover rate.
- Cost of HR communications or publications to staff.
- HR staff professional development and travel costs.
- Other changes in policy, business strategy, law, or regulation that may impact costs.
- HR revenue (via consulting, savings [from compensation, benefits, turnover reduction, training costs, etc.], rent, etc.).[6]

STRATEGIC MANAGEMENT RISK CHECKLIST

Interview key executives to determine whether HR has the support of senior management.
Review organizational strategic plan and HR strategic plan. • Is the senior HR director involved in the organization's strategic and operational planning process? • Does the HR strategic plan address major workforce issues to allow the organization to achieve its mission/goals/strategies? • Does the HR department's mission clearly describe the department's purpose within the organization?

STRATEGIC MANAGEMENT RISK CHECKLIST (Cont.)

Review HR operational plan. • Have the HR department's key result areas been identified? • Are the key result areas specifically assigned to positions within the HR department? • Is there a reasonable explanation if key HR result areas are instead assigned to positions or people outside the HR department? • Does HR identify and evaluate recommended strategies for vendor selection and/or outsourcing?
Determine how HR conducts ongoing performance assessment of the department (e.g., management reports, customer surveys, balanced scorecard). • Does HR have a process to improve activities based on performance assessment? • Have standards of performance or objectives been established for each HR department position? • Does HR calculate HR metrics to benchmark practices? • Does management agree that these benchmark practices indeed reflect key HR performance areas?
Review HR department budget. • Does the HR department budget indicate planned expenses by key result area, position, or other functional assignment? • Is the HR manager accountable for budget items required to analyze results and variances? • Conduct budget review to determine whether expenses are reasonable, properly recorded, and that adequate controls exist.
Does HR monitor the legislative and regulatory environment for proposed changes and the potential impact to the organization and take appropriate steps to support, modify, or oppose proposed changes?[7]

CHAPTER 2
DEPARTMENT STRUCTURE AND STAFF COMPETENCIES

There is no one correct way to organize an effective HR department. Some departments might be organized by function (e.g., employee relations, compensation, training) while others may be organized into more of a general service unit. It is important, however, that employees know where to go in HR for answers and that the HR department is perceived as "user friendly" rather than only as a "policing" function.

Sometimes a sign that management does not place sufficient trust in the HR department is a removal of HR functions to other departments. If an audit reveals that the HR department has been stripped of some core HR functions without a clear explanation or organizational need, then the HR leadership may be lacking.

The HR functions are so interrelated that it is vital that the HR leaders to have a broad strategic perspective. For example, changes to a performance appraisal system can have ripple effects through the compensation, training, discipline, and recruiting functions. Therefore, HR should not redesign any one particular function without first understanding the impact that the change could have on other areas.

This strategic perspective and understanding of the core HR functions is becoming more and more important for HR professionals. An organization needs knowledgeable HR staff with the professional competencies to perform their work at high standards. Unfortunately, many organizations continue to see HR as a simple administrative support function. This sometimes is reflected in HR staff that have moved up from more clerical positions and do not have specific HR professional knowledge.

The HR profession has placed considerable focus on the core competencies for HR staff. A SHRM 2007 survey[8] shows the following critical skills for HR professionals:

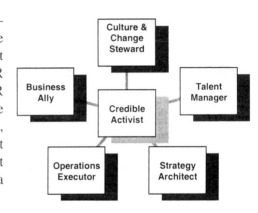

Credible Activist — Being a "credible activist" is the most critical skill for HR professionals. HR professionals need to be "trusted, respected, admired, listened to, but above all, have a point of view and take a position."[9]

Culture and Change Steward — Involves implementing strategy, projects, or initiatives that help turn what is known into what is done.

Talent Manager, Organization Designer — Deals with how workers move in, through, and out of the organization, as well as with the structure and culture of how the organization works.

Strategy Architect — Requires a vision of how the organization is moving forward and playing an active part in establishing overall strategy to deliver that vision.

Operational Executor — Ability to develop, implement, and efficiently deliver workforce-related programs.

Business Ally — Knowledge of the arenas in which their organization operates, the organization's mission, how profits are made, and who are the customers or clients.

STRUCTURE AND STAFF COMPETENCIES RISK CHECKLIST

Review HR department organizational chart.
- Is HR staff appropriately utilized?
- Is there one position in the HR department accountable for the management of the entire HR function?
- On what organizational level is the senior management position of the HR department placed?
- What percentage of HR department positions is currently filled?
- What is the annual employee turnover rate for the HR department?
- Do employees know whom to contact regarding specific HR activities?

Review staff competencies and continuing education.
- Does each HR department position have a written description with defined responsibilities or tasks, authorities, and competencies or requirements?
- Does HR staff have appropriate education, experience, and training to perform duties?
- Is HR staff encouraged to pursue continuing education and become members of professional associations?
- Does the organization pay for professional association dues and conference registrations for HR department employees?
- Are professional journals and magazines purchased and routed to all HR department employees?
- Are HR department employees encouraged to obtain professional certification in subjects for which certification is available (e.g., PHR, SPHR, CCP, CEBS)?
- Are HR positions compensated at appropriate levels to provide necessary service?

CHAPTER 3
HR FACILITIES

Auditors may want to conduct a basic review of the HR department's facility. This review may reveal some risk factors relating to the physical office space used by the HR function.

HR FACILITIES RISK CHECKLIST

Have the physical facilities of the HR department been designed for the work and the number of people involved?
Has an area been allocated for the reception of job candidates?
Is there a bulletin board in the area used for receiving candidates that contains all legal and other employment notices?
Are private areas available for interviews and employee consultations?
Is the HR area convenient to employees?
If there is HR voice mail, do messages include how to reach a live person?

CHAPTER 4
HR TECHNOLOGY AND INFORMATION CONTROL

HR and technology have become increasingly intertwined. In fact, data management is becoming an important part of the HR professional's skill set. The HR information system (HRIS) has become a vital tool that generates reports to assist in strategic and operational planning, as well as daily decision-making.

Lynne Mealy, president and chief executive officer of the International Association for Human Resource Information Management, says, "The technology infrastructure is now in place, and the key role for HR IT staff is no longer creating and maintaining systems but making sure the information and workflow meet their company's organizational objectives."[10]

HR is the owner of a variety of sensitive employment data. Therefore, risk controls are essential to safeguard this information.

HR TECHNOLOGY AND INFORMATION CONTROL RISK CHECKLIST

Determine what HRIS and other technology is installed.
- Does HR review and recommend application technology needs (e.g., HRIS, applicant tracking, employee and self-service technology)?
- Is technology up-to-date?
- Verify that appropriate backup and recovery procedures exist for HRIS.

HR TECHNOLOGY AND INFORMATION CONTROL RISK CHECKLIST (Cont.)

- Are there any important technology projects being developed?
- Test system security to make certain that employees have appropriate access to different levels of data.
- Review information management processes.
- Review a sample of management reports, tracing data to source system to verify accuracy of information.
- Are HR employees given training to deal appropriately with sensitive employee data?
- If an employee with access to the HR information system leaves the department, is that individual's access canceled, voided, or terminated?
- Discuss HR reports with management to see if they are satisfied with the accuracy, analysis, and timeliness of reports.
- Determine if any reports are being created that are not being reviewed and/or are unnecessary.

PART THREE
KEY HR RISK AREAS

An organization's human capital strategy should closely support the organizational strategy. HR systems are closely linked and changes in one system may create issues in another. Therefore, a broad view of how each HR system interrelates with the others is important when developing a strategic HR function. The graphic below represents the key HR functional areas:

CHAPTER 5
WORKFORCE PLANNING AND EMPLOYMENT

A common, if somewhat overused, definition of workforce planning is "to have the right number of people, with the right skills, at the right time to perform the required work." Workforce planning is a broad term that represents more than just staffing. It covers the full spectrum of moving talent in and out of an organization. To plan for an effective workforce, an organization must identify the number of workers and types of skill sets required to meet its strategic objectives.

Workforce Needs Determination

In order to truly understand its workforce needs, an organization should conduct an analysis of its current and future strategic, operating, and workforce plans to determine how its workforce needs are likely to change. A "supply analysis" provides information on the current workforce profile and what it needs to accomplish future organizational objectives. This analysis would include an employee demographic review and a skill profile. A "demand analysis" provides information on the future workforce needed by the organization. Finally, a "gap analysis" compares the current workforce projection and the demand forecast.

An auditor reviewing workforce planning efforts should focus on whether HR is performing adequate analyses and developing action plans to ensure the organization is not left with a serious shortage of qualified workers. Auditors should verify that HR has identified, and is utilizing, suitable recruiting sources that are capable of furnishing adequate numbers of qualified applicants for their organization.

Organizational Design

Organizational design is an essential process to structure work and to ensure that information flows as efficiently as possible.

Some key concepts in organizational design include[11]:

- Span of control
- Authority
- Responsibility
- Delegation
- Chain of command
- Accountability
- Line authority
- Staff departments

Usually, auditors will not spend much time reviewing organizational structures. A basic review to discover any "red flags" is usually sufficient. Examples of red flags may include: First-line supervisors with spans of control too great to be practicable (usually greater than 1:15); middle managers with lines of authority over only one other manager; chains of command that are not clearly designated or that reflect multiple, conflicting reporting relationships.

Recruiting Programs

HR departments often spend a significant percentage of their total staff time recruiting candidates for job vacancies. Sometimes an organization will have one or more dedicated recruiters focused on this effort. Recruiting sources can be varied depending on the types of positions that need to be filled and include: online job boards, newspapers, professional publications, and campus recruitment. Sometimes HR will contract with an employment agency to assist in recruiting efforts. Auditors may look for cost/benefit analyses of using such agencies. Since federal regulations require equal employment opportunity in hiring, organizations need to be able to recruit diverse applicant pools.

Chapter 5: Workforce Planning and Employment 25

Organizations are also required to keep applicant flow records in order to demonstrate that they are, in fact, attracting diverse applicant pools and they may be required to meet the goals of an established affirmative action plan. Usually, organizations are required to submit applicant flow reports to appropriate federal and/or state oversight agencies. Auditors should review applicant flow information to ensure that HR staff is properly documenting applicant information in an accurate and timely manner, and that records are current and available for appropriate review.

Selection Process

In most organizations, both hiring managers and HR play a part in selecting final candidates. In many cases, a selection panel makes the decision. There are several risks that can occur in the selection process, including permitting untrained managers to ask illegal questions, requiring applicant tests that are invalid and/or illegal, and documenting inappropriate reasons for selection or non-selection.

In addition, management can make discriminatory decisions in the hiring process. Therefore, it is important for the auditor to ensure that HR has trained the hiring managers in the basic principles of employment law. In many organizations, HR staff is required to attend an annual HR law seminar, in which legal experts explain any recent updates in employment law and conduct refresher training and exercises for attendees. It is then HR's responsibility to pass along critical legal updates to hiring managers.

Contractor Management

While the largest part of building a workforce involves hiring employees, many organizations also use independent contractors or contracted services to do specialized work that is for a short duration or project or where current employees do not have the necessary expertise. HR should ensure controls are in place to monitor theses individuals or service providers. Organizations should also routinely check independent contractor duties to ensure they meet the IRS requirements.

Succession Planning

Succession planning is the process of identifying and preparing suitable employees to replace incumbents in key positions. Though it is often touted as a best practice to ensure a smooth transition and limited downtime, not all organizations develop formal succession plans.

Turnover and Employee Retention

Just as workers come into an organization, eventually they must leave. HR has a vital role in analyzing employee turnover. Some turnover is a good thing, as it can help an organization bring in employees with new ideas and move employees with performance problems out of the organization. However, when turnover gets too high, the organization feels the stress of worker shortage and "churn," which decreases productivity.

Some sources state that turnover costs at least 150% of an employee's salary; therefore, organizations should pay attention to the causes of turnover. Exit interviews are a good tool for determining causes of turnover. Many studies suggest that dissatisfaction with a supervisor is a primary reason that employees terminate. For that reason, HR should not be the sole owner of employee retention programs since management plays such an important role.

Fraud

There are many situations that could involve employee fraud, from lying on an employment application to stealing coworkers' possessions. A glaring example is that the National Insurance Crime Bureau states that workers' compensation fraud is the largest form of insurance fraud. Some sources state that fraud can account for up to 30% of workers' compensation costs.[12]

HR can play an important role in reducing an organization's fraud risk by implementing appropriate policies, developing sound hiring practices (including thorough background checks), and providing ongoing fraud education for employees.

WORKFORCE PLANNING AND EMPLOYMENT RISK ASSESSMENT MATRIX

WORKFORCE NEEDS DETERMINATION

Obtain copy of workforce plan or other documents that describe how the organization plans for workforce needs.

Review documents to determine whether:
- HR plays a key role in the workforce planning process.
- The workforce plan is linked to the organization's strategic mission.
- Current and future workforce profiles are developed and gap analysis is performed. Are there any critical skills shortages?
- Workforce demographics reveal any unusual data trends.
- HR has performed environmental scans to determine impact on workforce.
- HR has forecast the number and specified positions that need to be filled.
- The projected staff requirements are used in planning recruitment activities and training and development programs to be offered.

WORKFORCE PLANNING AND EMPLOYMENT RISK ASSESSMENT MATRIX (Cont.)

ORGANIZATIONAL DESIGN   Obtain copy of overall organization chart.
Review organizational design process to determine whether: • Organizational chart has clearly defined roles and reporting relationships.   • The HR department provides expertise in ensuring the organizational structure supports the organization's mission.   • Procedures are in place to identify and resolve any organizational conflicts among departments.
EMPLOYMENT AND RECRUITMENT
Review the process for identifying job vacancies to determine whether: • HR is informed of all job vacancies within the organization.   • HR reviews job vacancy notices prior to posting.   • Job postings are developed from a current position description or recent job analysis.
Obtain recruitment action plans to determine whether they include budgets and time lines for addressing job vacancies and/or new positions.
Determine whether HR has developed a "branding" campaign to market the organization to applicants.
Review EEO/diversity plan regarding recruitment goals.
Determine whether the recruitment sources used are appropriate and adequate to produce a qualified and diverse applicant pool.
Review candidate screening process to ensure that appropriate screening techniques are used.
Determine whether the organization measures recruiting effectiveness by tracking and evaluating recruited employees and the total dollar costs of different recruiting methods.

WORKFORCE PLANNING AND EMPLOYMENT RISK ASSESSMENT MATRIX (Cont.)

Determine whether recruitment sources are periodically evaluated to ensure that they are meeting the needs of the organization (may review recruiting metrics such as time-to-fill or cost-per-hire).
SELECTION PROCESS
If the organization uses a standardized scoring tool (such as a selection matrix) to rank applicants on required job elements, does HR review the tool to ensure it is appropriate and legal?
Determine whether any applicants are tested (e.g., typing, psychological/personality, cognitive, assessment center, motor/physical assessment) as part of the selection process. If so, does HR review all tests to ensure their reliability and validity?
Determine whether employees who interview candidates have been trained in the types of questions and actions that are legal to ask in the hiring process.
Determine whether controls exist to ensure that all documentation of the recruitment and selection process is available, accurate, and complete. (This includes applications, resumes, test results, interview questions, recruiting summary, and so forth.)
Determine whether HR reviews minimum job qualifications to ensure that they are job related.
Determine whether controls exist to ensure that all applicants who are hired meet the posted minimum qualifications of the position.
Determine whether relocation procedures are consistently applied.
Ensure final selection decision is thoroughly documented. (This includes reasons for hiring versus not hiring.)
Determine whether "no offer" (rejection) letters are sent to all applicants. (While there is no legal requirement for organizations to do this, it is a good business etiquette practice.)

WORKFORCE PLANNING AND EMPLOYMENT RISK ASSESSMENT MATRIX (Cont.)

Make certain that background checks are conducted on all applicants to verify information reported in the application (e.g., prior employment history, education, certification/license).
Ensure that reference checks are conducted before an offer is made.
Ensure that criminal background checks are conducted on all applicants for positions of a sensitive nature (e.g., handling money; direct contact with children, elderly, or disabled; access to controlled substances) and that the results are received before a final offer is made. • Criminal history involving violence, theft, and fraud. • Civil history for lawsuits involving collections, restraining orders, and fraud. • Driver's license check for numerous or serious violations.[13]
Determine whether any required applicant drug tests are conducted if appropriate for the position (e.g., truck drivers, medical staff). Is the drug testing policy consistently applied? Are drug tests performed and results received before a final offer is made?
CONTRACTOR MANAGEMENT
Review workforce contracts and independent contractor management controls to ensure that the organization has: • Developed comprehensive policies and procedures. • Examined relevant legal and personnel issues. • Conducted cost-benefit analyses. • Documented how contract workers fit into their staffing strategies. • Review independent contractor work to ensure it meets IRS rules.

WORKFORCE PLANNING AND EMPLOYMENT RISK ASSESSMENT MATRIX (Cont.)

SUCCESSION PLANNING
Determine whether a succession plan for key positions has been developed. Review succession plan to determine whether: • Management succession chart was considered in making promotion decisions. • Multiple possible replacements have been identified for all key positions. • Employees that have been identified as replacements for other positions are provided with training and development to prepare them in advance for such positions. • Rotational assignments are used to prepare employees identified as replacements for other positions. • Development objectives are assigned to individual employees identified as replacements for other positions.
TURNOVER AND EMPLOYEE RETENTION
Determine whether the HR department has controls in place to ensure that supervisors and managers consult with a HR representative before employees are suspended or fired.
Review the process for terminating employees. • Determine whether retention programs have been developed and are owned by both management and HR. • Determine whether exit interviews or exit surveys are conducted with all employees who are voluntarily terminated. • Determine whether HR analyzes and takes actions on important issues brought out by the exit interviews or surveys. • Determine whether HR computes employee turnover rate, reasons for turnover, and related replacement costs. Review reports.

WORKFORCE PLANNING AND EMPLOYMENT RISK ASSESSMENT MATRIX (Cont.)

REGULATION COMPLIANCE
Review hiring policies and procedures to determine whether: - Recruitment and selection processes are supported by written policies and procedures that are updated, accurate, and complete. - Managers and interviewers are provided resources regarding recruitment and selection laws and regulations. - There are formal Equal Employment Opportunity (EEO) guidelines for recruitment and selection. - Federal EEO reports are submitted as required (see www.eeoc.gov/employers/surveys.html). - Employment Eligibility Verification forms (I-9) are completed for all new employees within three business days from the time of hire. - Applicant data for those not hired are retained for two years. - Hiring area has a bulletin board with all legally required notices on display. (See **Appendix B**.)
FRAUD
Ensure adequate internal controls are in place, including: - Separation of duties. - Access controls. - Authorization controls.[14]
Ensure employees are educated regarding fraud. Every employee should sign a form to verify receipt of fraud policy and code of ethics. Employees should receive annual training on these topics and on the definition of what is considered fraudulent behavior, and sign an acknowledgment each time.
Ensure that an anonymous fraud reporting system exists and that the system is promoted to employees.[15]

CHAPTER 6
HUMAN RESOURCES DEVELOPMENT

An effective training and development program is essential to ensure that employees have the necessary skills and knowledge to perform their jobs. An organization's training program provides new employees with a general understanding of an organization's culture and policies and procedures, provides staff with ongoing technical training, and ensures supervisors are trained to manage employees effectively. In today's environment of the "knowledge organization" there is a constant need to update skills and refresh knowledge.

Training System

Despite its value, training has notoriously been one of the first programs to be cut in a budget crunch. However, a decrease in training programs can have a direct impact on performance and ultimately on an organization's bottom line. An auditor's focus in the training area should be on whether HR is monitoring the training needs of the organization and making adjustments, and that the appropriate level of training for different positions is being offered.

One of the greatest risks for an organization is having untrained supervisors. Supervisors have the bulk of the frontline interaction with employees. Organizations do not discriminate or harass employees, people do. Yet many organizations do not take the important step to require new supervisors and managers to attend training on basic management principles and employment law.

Performance Management

Every day, supervisors must manage their employees so they will perform their jobs effectively. Effective coaching, therefore, is one of the most important management skills. Performance management does not just include performance appraisals, but also the full spectrum of managing an employee's job performance, including the daily process of providing feedback.

Performance appraisal systems are beneficial because they can communicate strategic vision, recognize valued performers, communicate improvement areas, ensure consistency, and distinguish between employees' performance.

Employee performance appraisal programs are intended to:

- Measure work performance as compared to job expectations.
- Provide feedback and counseling.
- Determine employees' and management's goals.
- Identify employees' developmental needs.
- Provide documentation for future actions.
- Allocate rewards and opportunities.

There are many perspectives on what makes a good performance appraisal system or how the appraisal form should be constructed. There is even one school of thought that believes performance appraisals should be discarded.[16] However, the majority of organizations continue to have a formal appraisal system to assess employee performance. Important issues to consider during an audit are whether appraisals are done in a timely manner, are based on job-specific criteria, and do not document information that could be considered discriminatory.

As part of assessing an employee performance system, auditors may want to pay attention to some of the reasons performance appraisals are often criticized:

- **Deficiency** — Does not adequately measure all aspects of the job.
- **Contamination** — Items unrelated to job performance are evaluated.
- **Evaluation Errors** — Is not specific, objective, accurate, or consistent.
- **Past Focus** — Used to rate past performance, rather than to improve future performance.
- **Non-use** — If people do not use it, you do not have a system.

Counseling and Discipline

While most of a manager's time is spent coaching and overseeing employees' performance, there are still times when performance problems may occur. When they do, managers need to be able to quickly assess the problem and help the employee's performance improve or move toward disciplinary actions.

When an employee's performance slips below what is expected, supervisors need a process to formally correct performance. Most organizations will have some type of procedure to formally counsel the employee or put them into a "performance improvement plan."

A performance or conduct issue may eventually require stronger corrective action in the form of some type of discipline. Many organizations have a progressive discipline process that states that employees may be subject to increasing levels of discipline (e.g., oral warning, written warning, suspension with pay, suspension without pay, termination).

Of concern to the auditor is verifying that management has appropriately documented the performance problem and action taken, including acknowledgement that the employee was made aware of the problem. This is an important risk area since disciplined employees may file an internal grievance or external complaint and/or lawsuit. Management's documentation should be able to support the decision made since it could be subject to further scrutiny.

HUMAN RESOURCE DEVELOPMENT RISK ASSESSMENT MATRIX

TRAINING NEEDS ASSESSMENT
Review process for how organization develops training plan. Is the training program reactive in nature (based on employee or manager requests) or proactive (interviews with managers regarding needed skill improvement, performance appraisal reviews, employee surveys).
Determine whether training staff performs cost benefit analysis of different internal delivery methods (i.e., classroom, individual coaching, Web-based training, and rotational job assignments) that are used for training.
Review training information system to determine if there is a single automated system that maintains information on external courses and seminars attended.
Obtain any training catalogues or listings for available internal and external training.
NEW EMPLOYEE TRAINING
Review new employee orientation schedules to ensure that all employees attended orientation within reasonable time frame (usually no more than first 30 days of employment).

HUMAN RESOURCE DEVELOPMENT
RISK ASSESSMENT MATRIX (Cont.)

Review new employee orientation outline to determine whether the following issues are covered: • Insurance and benefits information • Grievance policy • Disciplinary action policy • Safety and security issues • Worker's compensation • Performance appraisal process • Sexual harassment issues • Employee leave policies • Americans with Disabilities Act • Equal employment opportunity-related topics • Privacy, information security, and technology
TECHNICAL TRAINING
Review technical training program(s) to determine whether: • Skill-based training programs are available for skills sets unique to the organization. • Training programs have clearly established and specific behavioral objectives. • Employees who deliver training or outside trainers are required to be knowledgeable in the contents of the programs they deliver. • Employees who deliver training have received train-the-trainer instruction.
Determine if the organization offers a tuition reimbursement program and, if so, review the policy to determine whether: • Courses or course of study are related to the employee's current job. • Reimbursement is based on achieving a certain grade.

HUMAN RESOURCE DEVELOPMENT RISK ASSESSMENT MATRIX (Cont.)

SUPERVISOR TRAINING
Determine whether employees that are newly promoted or hired into a supervisory position are required to attend management training in a reasonable time frame (usually no more than the first 90 days after promotion/hire).
Review the supervisory training course outline schedule to determine whether the following issues are covered: • Basic management principals • Employment law • How to deal with employee issues • Employee performance management
TRAINING ASSESSMENT
Review the organization's process for assessing the value of training programs to determine whether: • The results of training programs are continually monitored and evaluated (e.g., surveys, pre- and post-testing). • The results of training are compared to the training program's behavioral objectives. • Follow-up reviews are regularly conducted with managers of employees attending training programs to determine the results as reflected on the job. • The subject matter of training programs is regularly reviewed with the managers of the areas for which the training is conducted. • The costs of training in each program are regularly calculated.
EMPLOYEE COACHING
Supervisors should be trained in performance management techniques, including how to recognize and address employee problems. Verify that training is required on a regular basis.

HUMAN RESOURCE DEVELOPMENT
RISK ASSESSMENT MATRIX (Cont.)

PERFORMANCE APRAISAL

Review performance appraisal policies and procedures.
- Verify that employees receive formal performance appraisals on at least an annual basis.
- If the organization has a formal probationary period, determine if employees are consistently appraised before the end of the period.
- Obtain copy of all performance appraisal forms used. Review appraisal forms to determine whether appraisals are based on specific job-related criteria rather than employee behaviors or personal traits.
- Review sample of completed performance appraisals to determine if form was completed within time stated by policy (usually annually); employee has signed form indicating the form was discussed with them; supervisor comments are job-specific and appropriate. Generally, supervisor comments should not refer to an employee's medical issues or time away from work if granted to comply with state or federal law (family and medical leave, leave associated with a disability, worker's compensation leave).
- Determine if HR reviews performance ratings and supervisor support/comments for inconsistencies across the organization.
- Determine whether HR tracks and monitors appraisal due dates and notifies supervisors.
- Review whether supervisors are held accountable for timely evaluations (is it a criteria in the supervisor's performance appraisal?).

HUMAN RESOURCE DEVELOPMENT RISK ASSESSMENT MATRIX (Cont.)

COUNSELING
Review performance improvement/counseling policy and procedures. • Determine whether HR is notified when a supervisor counsels an employee and puts him/her on a performance improvement plan. Verify that HR tracks all employees on formal performance improvement plans and monitors deadlines with supervisor. • Determine whether HR reviews trends in performance problems and feeds this information into training programs when appropriate. • Review sample of documentation regarding employees in performance improvement plans to ensure appropriate support, action plan, employee acknowledgment, and final settlement is documented. • Determine whether there is an HR professional assigned to counsel employees on personal problems. Are procedures in place to ensure the confidentiality of employee discussions? Has the individual conducting the counseling been trained in appropriate techniques? • Determine whether an external employee assistance program (EAP) is available for employees. Review how employees are notified of EAP services and how to contact the provider.
DISCIPLINE
Review disciplinary action policy and procedures. • Obtain list from HR of disciplinary actions. HR should track all employee discipline actions and have documentation of performance or conduct issue, management steps taken, and final outcome of action.

HUMAN RESOURCE DEVELOPMENT
RISK ASSESSMENT MATRIX (Cont.)

- Review sample of disciplinary actions to ensure proper support, action steps, and employee acknowledgment are documented. Determine if disciplinary actions appear consistent for similar problems across the organization.

CHAPTER 7
TOTAL REWARDS

Employee rewards are one of the most complex HR systems. A handbook on general HR auditing cannot go into the depth needed to conduct a comprehensive compensation audit. Auditors may wish to work with a compensation expert when reviewing this area.

Organizations often have specific and unique components of their reward systems. However, a traditional reward system includes both cash and non-cash rewards. A reward system should help support the organization's strategic mission, motivate employees, and reward performance. Compensation systems should be both externally competitive and provide internal equity.

Compensation Philosophy

The first step in establishing a system is to develop a compensation philosophy. A compensation philosophy will define how the organization wants to pay people with respect to its position in the labor market (i.e., lead, lag, or meet salaries paid by competing organizations). A philosophy also helps give managers and employees a clearer understanding of the organization's position on compensation.

Base Pay Program

After a philosophy has been developed, the next step is to set up a base pay program. To design a base pay system, an organization must complete these four main steps:

- Job documentation
- Market analysis

- Salary structure development
- Job evaluation

Job documentation requires HR to review all jobs and create specific job descriptions that define the duties and responsibilities, as well as the skills and education needed for each specific position. Job descriptions serve as a key foundation for many different HR systems, including compensation system design, recruitment, and performance appraisals. Therefore, they should be taken seriously. Written, updated job descriptions should be available for all positions.

When conducting a **market analysis**, the first step is to define the organization's competitive market. Organizations should consider various factors such as the industry, geographic location, total employment, and annual revenue. It is also important to consider not only business competitors, but people competitors as well — other organizations where the organization gets and loses talent.[17] After defining the competitive market, an assessment is made of market pay for jobs performing similar work. This is usually done through salary surveys.

Once the market analysis is completed, an organization can develop a **salary structure**. A salary structure helps an organization manage pay. The structure typically includes several salary ranges or bands that include a minimum and maximum salary rate.

Finally, jobs are grouped into ranges or bands based on a **job evaluation system**. There are many types of evaluation systems, but their goal of all systems is to group jobs of similar value into the same range or band.

Differential pay (e.g., FLSA overtime, shift differentials, geographical differentials, longevity pay, on-call pay, hazardous duty pay) can also factor into an employee's base pay.

Salary Administration

Once the general structure of pay has been developed, organizations must manage salary administration throughout an employee's career. Salary administration is a broad term that covers any action that impacts an individual employee's pay and can include merit increases, variable performance pay, promotions, bonuses, stock options, and deferred compensation, to name a few.

FLSA Determinations and Overtime

A key area of risk for organizations is appropriately complying with the Fair Labor Standards Act (FLSA) regarding overtime pay. Organizations must correctly classify each position as non-exempt (subject to overtime pay) or exempt (not subject to overtime pay). In addition, they must correctly calculate overtime pay for non-exempt employees.

HR should be performing regular checks of their FLSA determinations and overtime policies to ensure compliance with the law.

Benefits Administration

Organizations also offer other non-cash rewards or incentives usually described as employee benefits. Benefit programs often include: medical insurance, life insurance, vacation and leave policies, and some form of organization-sponsored retirement or savings plan. Factors to consider in developing benefit plans are external competitiveness, cost effectiveness, employee needs and preferences, and compliance with state and federal laws.

Payroll

Making sure that employees are paid timely and correctly is an integral part of an organization's stability. The payroll function may be a part of the HR department or it may be part of the finance department. Payroll staff is responsible for ensuring new hires, personnel actions, work hours, and differential pay are efficiently processed so that paychecks are accurate. The payroll function is sometimes audited as part of a larger financial audit.

TOTAL REWARDS RISK ASSESSMENT MATRIX

COMPENSATION PHILOSOPHY
Obtain copy of written compensation philosophy.
Determine whether the compensation philosophy is clearly communicated to all employees and supervisors.
Determine whether employees receive written policies and procedures regarding the overall compensation administration program.
JOB DOCUMENTATION
Review to ensure that all positions have job descriptions.
Review sample of current position descriptions to ensure that essential job duties, knowledge, skills, abilities, education, and experience are appropriate for job. Ensure that job descriptions do not have physical requirements that are not essential to the job (Americans with Disabilities Act violation).
Determine whether positions have functional job descriptions that describe the unique position rather than just a broad classification description.
Determine how often functional job descriptions are reviewed for currency and accuracy.

TOTAL REWARDS
RISK ASSESSMENT MATRIX (Cont.)

Review the process of how employees are notified of their job title and description.
MARKET ANALYSIS
Review procedure for analysis of position salaries compared to the market. Are compensation surveys conducted or purchased for the geographic area or industry? How does the organization take action on positions that significantly lead or lag the market?
SALARY STRUCTURE DEVELOPMENT
Determine whether the organization uses a salary structure with established salary grades and ranges within grades. If a structure is used, review to ensure that: • Structure fully encompasses all employee salaries (i.e., employees are not paid below minimum or above maximum of salary grade range. If employee is paid outside of range, this should be based on a recent salary structure change and the procedures should be in place to quickly move within the structure). • HR uses a process to analyze salary structure for market competitiveness and/or cost of living adjustments and make adjustments. How often is the structure reviewed? • HR staff or contracted vendor has appropriate compensation expertise to perform salary structure review.
JOB EVALUATION
Determine whether a thorough job analysis is conducted on new positions to place them in correct title and level.
Determine whether HR has process to review positions to ensure internal salary equity of positions across the organization.
Determine whether there is a process for employees to request a review of their position if they believe they are misclassified in an incorrect title or level.

TOTAL REWARDS
RISK ASSESSMENT MATRIX (Cont.)

Determine whether HR staff or contracted vendor has appropriate compensation expertise to perform job evaluation analysis.

SALARY ADMINISTRATION

Review salary administration procedures.
- Determine whether specific guidelines are provided to supervisors for salary adjustments.
- Determine whether promotions and pay for performance increases are supported by documented justification.
- Determine whether executive compensation programs are appropriately administered (e.g., stock purchase, stock options, incentive, bonus, supplemental retirement plan).
- Determine whether expatriate and foreign national reward systems are appropriately administered.
- Determine whether HR reviews salary actions to ensure they are nondiscriminatory.

FLSA DETERMINATIONS AND OVERTIME

Review process for how the Fair Labor Standards Act (FLSA) exempt or nonexempt status is determined for each position.

Obtain policies and procedures regarding FLSA overtime compensation requirements.

Test sample of FLSA determinations for compliance with regulations.

Test sample of timesheets for appropriate overtime calculations.

EMPLOYEE BENEFITS

Obtain copy of employee benefits program.
- Review to ensure that benefit program applies to all employees.
- Review to ensure that benefits information is communicated to employees.
- Determine whether HR conducts benefit program need assessments.

TOTAL REWARDS
RISK ASSESSMENT MATRIX (Cont.)

• Review benefits enrollment process. • Review process for filing claims, challenging benefits determinations, and changing coverages.
Review paid leave policies and procedures. • Test sample of paid leave calculations to ensure procedures are followed consistently.
Review retirement plan. • Are all employees allowed to participate? • Is the vesting period the same for all employees?
PAYROLL
Review HR process for communicating payroll information (e.g., new hires, deductions, adjustments, terminations).
Test to ensure that payroll master file has accurate employee data.
Review to ensure appropriate controls are in place to approve payroll file changes.
Determine whether access to payroll file data is restricted to authorized staff. Is automated payroll data safeguarded with appropriate security controls?
Determine whether monthly reconciliations between payroll file and accounting records are performed
Determine whether preliminary payroll report is checked against previous month to detect any significant deviations.
Assess whether payroll file is monthly reconciled against tax reporting.
Ensure that all employees have accurate payroll deduction calculations.
Review to determine whether supplemental payrolls are not used to regularly process regular payroll mistakes or oversights.
Test to determine whether terminated employees final payments are accurately calculated.

CHAPTER 8
EMPLOYEE AND LABOR RELATIONS

A large portion of HR administration deals with the processes related to managing employees throughout their careers with an organization. There are several employment risk events including[18]:

- Discrimination.
- Harassment.
- Wrongful discharge.
- Negligent hiring, retention, and supervision.
- Defamation.
- Employee privacy.

Employee Handbook

The first step in establishing effective employee management processes is to have comprehensive policies and procedures that address any work situation. Most organizations use an employee handbook to centrally locate employment policies and procedures. An intranet/online policies and procedures handbook is useful, since employees and managers can be assured that they have a copy of the most recent version.

Employee Attitude Surveys

Employee attitude surveys can be useful management tools to help gather information on some specific issues and to show staff that they have a "voice" in affecting organization policies. One of the most important tasks of management is to take action based on any survey results. Otherwise surveying can actually decrease morale, as employees lose faith that their opinion actually matters.

Employment Files

For organizational and legal purposes, HR should maintain an employment file on each employee. In today's environment, some employment files are kept electronically; however, many organizations still keep hard copy personnel files. Files should include:

- **Employment information** — resume, application, and W-4 forms.
- **Job history data** — job description(s), promotion documentation.
- **Performance information** — appraisal forms, counseling notes, performance improvement plans.
- **Additional information** — relating to policies and procedures is often kept in files.
- **Training certificates of completion.**

Separate files should be kept regarding employee medical information. Employment eligibility forms (I-9) and supporting documentation should also be kept in separate files. It is an important HR practice to ensure security of employment files.

Employee Relations

The process of how an organization handles employee complaints and grievances can be an important area for auditors. This is an area where a clear "audit trail" is necessary. HR should track employee complaints and grievances — documentation should include the date, situation, and nature of the grievance or complaint; the action management has taken; any investigation results; and the final outcome or settlement. There should be a process for employees to express complaints and grievances to management and timely and thorough response from management.

Labor Relations

If an organization has a labor agreement, then policy changes, attitude surveys, and employee complaints and grievances have an added element of review and negotiation.

EMPLOYEE AND LABOR RELATIONS RISK MANAGEMENT MATRIX

POLICIES AND PROCEDURES
Obtain employee handbook.
Review policies and procedures to ensure appropriate coverage and that they are in compliance with federal and state regulations and consistently applied.
Review process for how often policies and procedures are reviewed and updated. (NOTE: If policies and procedures are kept online, HR should keep an historical file of dated past policies. This is helpful if there is an employee grievance or performance issue and the policy has changed since the time of the incident.)
Review HR's process for answering questions, addressing concerns about employee relations issues, and discussing work-related and/or personnel practices.
Determine whether the organization has a supervisor guide to employment regulations. This is a very good risk management tool, but it is not a common HR practice.
Review employee relations/retention programs (e.g., awards, events, discounts other types of recognition).
EMPLOYEE ATTITUDE SURVEYS
Obtain recent employee attitude surveys and reports. Determine how often employee attitude surveys are conducted.
Review survey process to determine whether confidentiality of employees' responses is assured.

EMPLOYEE AND LABOR RELATIONS RISK MANAGEMENT MATRIX (Cont.)

Review process of how survey results are shared with management and employees.
Determine whether management has procedures in place to take action on issues raised in the survey.
EMPLOYEE RECORDS
Review personnel file procedures.
Test to ensure that all employee records are kept in a secured location with controlled access.
Review to ensure that all employee records are kept in an environmentally safe location (i.e., fire, water, insect-proof).
Test to determine whether all employee medical information, including family and medical leave and disability accommodation requests, is kept in files separate from general personnel file.
Test to determine whether all Employment Eligibility Verification (I-9) forms and any other documentation identifying EEO data are kept separate from general personnel file.
Test sample of I-9 forms to ensure appropriate documentation is provided and submitted within three days of hire.
Test sample of personnel files to ensure files include complete and appropriate information.
Determine whether employee records are retained for four years.
EMPLOYEE COMPLAINT AND GRIEVANCE PROCESSES
Obtain and review grievance procedures. Are procedures in place for the identification, documentation, investigation, and final resolution of problems throughout the grievance process? Does the organization monitor the number of discrimination and harassment charges?

EMPLOYEE AND LABOR RELATIONS RISK MANAGEMENT MATRIX (Cont.)

Determine whether HR has controls in place to ensure that they are aware of all employee complaints. Are employee complaints monitored and evaluated in order to highlight potential areas of concern?
Ensure that all employee complaints and grievances and related documentation are filed in a secure location.
Determine whether HR analyzes the causes of complaints and grievances and makes recommendations for corrective and preventive measures to reduce the number of complaints and grievances filed.
Determine if there is any outstanding litigation.
LABOR RELATIONS
Review collective bargaining agreements and determine when they expire.
Gain understanding of what unions exist that impact the organization and which of the organization's jobs are covered.
Determine whether HR participates in collective bargaining activities, including contract negotiation and administration.

CHAPTER 9
RISK MANAGEMENT

In many organizations, HR may not have the full responsibility for risk management. However, HR usually has involvement in employee safety and health programs. "With the surge of worker's compensation expenses across the country and Title VII, ADA, wrongful termination exposure, and other compliance issues, the risk function has begun to overlap with safety and HR more than ever before. The "people risk" is exposing companies to more liability than the traditional areas of risk management."[19]

An effective safety and health program depends on the credibility of management's involvement in the program; inclusion of employees in safety and health decisions; rigorous worksite analysis to identify hazards and potential hazards, including those which could result from a change in worksite conditions or practices; stringent prevention and control measures; and thorough training.[20]

RISK MANAGEMENT MATRIX

SAFETY AND HEALTH
Review workplace health, safety, and security plans.
Determine whether HR participates in enterprise risk management by conducting self-assessments of HR policies and procedures to identify potential risk. • Does HR have a method of quantifying to management the dollars of exposure the organization may have from discrimination risks?

RISK MANAGEMENT MATRIX (Cont.)

• Are HR managers advising management how much money to reserve to pay or defend employment claims? • Does HR track historical employment losses to measure the success of the employment practices? • If the organization decided to purchase employment practices liability coverage, could the HR department provide a five year loss history, including legal expenses, settlement payments and investigations costs?[21]
Review worker's compensation data reports and safety incident reports.
Determine whether HR has established privacy policies (e.g., identity theft, data protection, HIPAA compliance).
Review business continuity and disaster recovery plans. Are these plans communicated to managers and employees?

PART FOUR
HR SERVICES OUTSOURCING AND CO-SOURCING

Over the past few years, many organizations have outsourced one or more HR services. A recent survey states that many organizations "expect to expand HR outsourcing across the board, with significant increases in the following areas: leave management, learning and development, payroll, recruiting, health and welfare, defined benefit plans, and global mobility."[22] Fully outsourcing a function is not always the best fit, so many organizations have moved to "co-sourcing," which is more of a partnership between the HR function and a service provider.

With HR outsourcing and co-sourcing becoming so prevalent, the HR audit must include a review of the contract administration process since an organization is trading HR administrative tasks for vendor management. HR must monitor the vendor's performance to ensure that the contractor is performing all duties in accordance with the contract so that the organization can be aware of and address any developing problems or issues.

Some organizations experience problems with the outsourcing process. Vendor problems include: poor execution, service level agreement performance, cost management, over-promising and under-delivering, inability to deliver purported global service capabilities, and turnover on the vendor's project team. Organizational issues include: underestimating the complexity of and time required for the outsourcing transition, organizational resistance to change, and IT compatibility issues."[23]

OUTSOURCING AND CO-SOURCING RISK ASSESSMENT MATRIX

VENDOR SELECTION PROCESS
Review the selection process of the vendor(s) and periodic fee negotiations. • Was the scope and nature of the work to be outsourced accurately described? • Were both HR professionals and non-HR professionals, such as budget analysts, contract managers, and others, involved in the proposal evaluation process? • Were competencies of the selected vendor, as well as best-value bid, appropriately considered when awarding the bid? • If a sole source contract was issued, has the selected vendor adequately demonstrated the ability to perform the contracted service for other organizations? • Does the contract have adequate non-performance clauses to enable the organization to void the contract in the event the vendor does not, or cannot, perform according to expectations? • Did the organization spend the time for due diligence and reference checking? • Did HR conduct a review of future workforce needs to ensure they would not outgrow the vendor's capabilities? • Did contract negotiations include sufficient service level agreements and guarantees/incentives? • Did HR consider putting some fees at risk?
VENDOR MANAGEMENT
HR should conduct an annual review of the outsourcing vendor(s)[24]: • Review the statement of work and other contract terms, including vendor compliance requirements. • Review vendor fees for appropriateness. • Consider site visit to vendor's place of business.

OUTSOURCING AND CO-SOURCING RISK ASSESSMENT MATRIX (Cont.)

- Compare the actual performance against the contract requirements. Is the vendor performing in accordance with the contract requirements?
- Compare actual expenditures to the approved budget. Is the vendor following their approved budget plan?
- Compare the current period to prior periods. Are there any unexplained trends? Is the vendor performing work significantly different from the last period?
- Review change orders for appropriateness and trends.

Review contract manager responsibilities and effectiveness.

APPENDIX A
HR METRICS

Strategic Management
- Revenue per FTE (full-time equivalent employee)
- Net income per FTE
- Salaries as a percentage of operating expense
- HR expenses to operating expense ratio
- HR staff to FTE ratio
- HR expense per FTE

Workforce Planning and Employment
- Recruitment and selection cost-per-hire
- Time-to-fill (average days needed to fill job vacancy)
- Ratio of applicants to job vacancy by job family
- Ratio of offers to applicants
- Ratio of applicants in protected classes to their representation in local labor market
- Ratio of offers made to applicants in protected classes to offers made to other applicants
- Ratio of acceptances to offers
- Ratio of open requisitions filled internally to openings filled externally
- Average test scores for new hires in applicable job families
- Percent of new hires per job family successfully completing probationary period

HR Development
- Training hours per FTE
- Training dollars per FTE
- Percent of employees receiving training in each job family
- Percent of employees receiving tuition refunds
- Average pre- and post-training test score change, if available

- Ratio of costs of training current employees to costs of recruiting outside applicants when filling vacancies
- Distribution of performance appraisal ratings

Total Rewards
- Average hourly cost of nonexempt employees, salaried employees, and independent contractors
- Ratio of average salary to midpoint by grade level (compa-ratio)
- Average merit pay increase per performance level
- Ratio of promotions to total employees
- Ratio of reclassified employees to total employees
- Ratio of overtime hours to regular hours
- Annual ratio of ex-employees citing pay as factor in leaving the company to total employees and to total ex-employees
- Ratio of wages earned by employees in protected classes to wages earned by other employees
- Benefit cost per FTE, per payroll dollar, per revenue dollar, per total operating budget
- Benefit cost as a percentage of base salaries
- Health care expense per FTE
- Health care expense per covered employees
- Percentage of premium organization pays for employee only coverage
- Percentage of premium organization pays for employee and dependent coverage
- Percentage of sick and vacation leave to total pay
- Average unemployment compensation payment and experience rating
- Average worker's compensation payment and experience rating
- Average annual worker's compensation and unemployment insurance premiums

Employee and Labor Relations
- Percent of managers seeking consultations with HR staff
- Percent of employees seeking advice from HR staff
- Average response time to inquiries
- Ratio of grievances or complaints to total FTEs
- Percent of grievances or complaints settled out-of-court and associated cost savings
- Average length of time to settle grievances or complaints
- Ratio of EEO grievances to total FTEs
- Lawsuit cost per FTE ratio
- Absenteeism rate overall and by department
- Minority representation by EEO categories
- Turnover rate overall and by department
- Ratio of voluntary to involuntary terminations
- Average employee tenure
- Ratio of successful to unsuccessful union drives
- Costs associated with work stoppages or slowdowns

Risk Management
- Frequency and severity of OSHA-reportable accidents
- Ratio of OSHA citations to total FTEs
- Ratio of safety-related expenses to total payroll

APPENDIX B
LEGALLY REQUIRED NOTICES

POSTER	WHO MUST POST	PENALTY
Job Safety and Health Protection	Private employers engaged in a business affecting commerce. Does not apply to federal, state, or political subdivisions of states.	Any covered employer failing to post the poster may be subject to citation and penalty.
Equal Employment Opportunity is the Law	Entities holding federal contracts or subcontracts or federally assisted construction contracts of $10,000 or more; financial institutions which are issuing and paying agents for U.S. savings bonds and savings notes; depositories of federal funds or entities having government bills of lading.	Appropriate contract sanctions may be imposed for uncorrected violations.

POSTER	WHO MUST POST	PENALTY
Federal Minimum Wage	Every private, federal, state, and local government employer employing any employee subject to the Fair Labor Standards Act, 29 USC 211, 29 CFR 5 16.4.	No citations or penalties for failure to post.
Notice to Workers With Disabilities Paid at Special Minimum Wages	Every employer having workers employed under special minimum wage certificates authorized by section 14(c) of the Fair Labor Standards Act.	No citations or penalties for failure to post.

POSTER	WHO MUST POST	PENALTY
Your Rights Under the Family and Medical Leave Act	Public agencies (including state, local, and federal employers), public and private elementary and secondary schools, as well as private sector employers who employ 50 or more employees in 20 or more work weeks and who are engaged in commerce or in any industry or activity affecting commerce, including joint employers and successors of covered employers.	Willful refusal to post may result in a civil money penalty by the Wage and Hour Division not to exceed $100 for each separate offense.

POSTER	WHO MUST POST	PENALTY
Uniformed Services Employment and Reemployment Rights Act	Each employer must provide the full text of the notice to persons entitled to rights and benefits under USERRA.	No citations or penalties for failure to notify. An individual could ask USDOL to investigate and seek compliance, or file a private enforcement action to require the employer to provide the notice to employees.
Notice to All Employees Working on Federal or Federally Financed Construction Projects	Any contractor/ subcontractor engaged in contracts in excess of $2,000 for the actual construction, alteration/repair of a public building or public work or building or work financed in whole or in part from federal funds, federal guarantee, or federal pledge which is subject to the labor standards provisions of any of the acts listed in 29 CFR 5.1.	No citations or penalties for failure to post.

POSTER	WHO MUST POST	PENALTY
Notice to Employees Working on Government Contracts	Every contractor or subcontractor engaged in a contract with the United States or the District of Columbia in excess of $2,500 the principal purpose of which is to furnish services in the U.S. through the use of service employees.	No citations or penalties for failure to post.
Notice: Employee Polygraph Protection Act	Any employer engaged in or affecting commerce or in the production of goods for commerce. Does not apply to federal, state, and local governments, or to circumstances covered by the national defense and security exemption.	The Secretary of Labor can bring court actions and assess civil penalties for failing to post.

POSTER	WHO MUST POST	PENALTY
Notice: Migrant and Seasonal Agriculture Worker Protection Act	Agricultural employers, agricultural associations, and farm labor contractors.	A civil money penalty may be assessed.

NOTE: Each state may have additional legally required employment postings.

APPENDIX C
KEY EMPLOYMENT REGULATIONS

Age Discrimination in Employment Act of 1967 (ADEA)

The ADEA protects employees and applicants who are 40 years of age or older from employment discrimination based on age. Under the ADEA, it is unlawful to discriminate against a person because of his/her age with respect to any term, condition, or privilege of employment — including, but not limited to, hiring, firing, promotion, layoff, compensation, benefits, job assignments, and training.

It is also unlawful to retaliate against an individual for opposing employment practices that discriminate based on age or for filing an age discrimination charge, testifying, or participating in any way in an investigation, proceeding, or litigation under the ADEA.

The ADEA applies to employers with 20 or more employees, including state and local governments. It also applies to employment agencies and to labor organizations, as well as to the federal government.

http://www.eeoc.gov/policy/adea.html

Americans with Disabilities Act of 1990 (ADA)

The ADA prohibits private employers, state and local governments, employment agencies and labor unions from discriminating against qualified individuals with disabilities in job application procedures, hiring, firing, advancement, compensation, job training, and other terms, conditions and privileges of employment. An individual with a disability is a person who:

- Has a physical or mental impairment that substantially limits one or more major life activities;
- Has a record of such an impairment; or
- Is regarded as having such an impairment.

An employer is required to make an accommodation to the known disability of a qualified applicant or employee if it would not impose an "undue hardship" on the operation of the employer's business. Undue hardship is defined as an action requiring significant difficulty or expense when considered in light of factors such as an employer's size, financial resources and the nature and structure of its operation.

http://www.dol.gov/dol/topic/disability/ada.htm

At-Will Employment

An at-will employee can be terminated at any time, and for any reason — or no reason at all.

Civil Rights Act of 1964 (Title VII)

Title VII prohibits discrimination in hiring, promotion, discharge, pay, fringe benefits, job training, classification, referral, and other aspects of employment, on the basis of race, color, religion, sex or national origin.

http://www.dol.gov/oasam/regs/statutes/2000e-16.htm

Equal Pay Act

The Equal Pay Act prohibits wage discrimination on the basis of sex. The Equal Pay Act's basic statutory provision is that an employer shall not discriminate between employees on the basis of sex by paying wages to employees at a rate less than the rate paid the opposite sex for equal work on jobs the performance of which requires equal skill, effort, and responsibility, and which are performed under similar working conditions, except where such payment is made pursuant to a seniority system, merit system, or quantity or quality of production system. Basically the Acts proscribe equal pay for equal work.

http://www.eeoc.gov/epa/

Fair Labor Standards Act (FLSA)

The FLSA establishes minimum wage, overtime pay, record-keeping and child labor standards for nearly all workers in the private sector and in federal, state and local governments.

http://www.dol.gov/dol/compliance/comp-flsa.htm

Family and Medical Leave Act (FMLA)

The FMLA provides covered employees with entitlement to up to 12 weeks of job-protected, unpaid leave during any 12 months for the following reasons:

- Birth and care of the employee's child or placement for adoption or foster care of a child with the employee;
- To care for an immediate family member (spouse, child, parent) who has a serious health condition; or
- For the employee's own serious health condition.

http://www.dol.gov/esa/whd/fmla/

Health Insurance Portability and Account. Act (HIPAA)

The HIPAA Privacy Rule creates national standards to protect individuals' medical records and other personal health information and to give patients more control over their health information. It sets limits on the use and release of health records. It establishes safeguards that providers and health plans must implement to protect the privacy of health information. The Privacy Rule provides that, in general, a covered entity may not use or disclose an individual's healthcare information without permission except for treatment, payment, or healtho Designate an individual to be responsible for seeing that privacy procedures are adopted and followed healthcare operations.

http://www.hhs.gov/ocr/hipaa/

Immigration Reform Control Act of 1986 (IRCA)

The IRCA was passed to control unauthorized immigration to the United States. Employer sanctions, increased appropriations for enforcement, and amnesty provisions of IRCA are the main ways of accomplishing its objective. The employer sanctions provision designates penalties for employers who hire aliens not authorized to work in the United States.

http://www.usda.gov/oce/oce/labor-affairs/ircasumm.htm

National Labor Relations Act (NLRA)

The NLRA states and defines the rights of employees to organize and to bargain collectively with their employers through representatives of their own choosing or not to do so. To ensure that employees can freely choose their own representatives for the purpose of collective bargaining, or choose not to be represented, the Act establishes a procedure by which they can exercise their choice at a secret-ballot election conducted by the NLRB. Further, to protect the rights of employees and employers, and to prevent labor disputes that would adversely affect the rights of the public, Congress has defined certain practices of employers and unions as unfair labor practices.

http://www.nlrb.gov/nlrb/legal/manuals/rules/act.asp

Occupational Safety and Health Act of 1970 (OSHA)

OSHA encourages employers and employees to reduce workplace hazards and to implement safety and health programs. In carrying out its duties, OSHA is responsible for promulgating legally enforceable standards. Where OSHA has not promulgated specific standards, employers "shall furnish a place of employment which is free from recognized hazards that are causing or are likely to cause death or serious physical harm to his employees."

http://www.osha.gov/

Pregnancy Discrimination Act (PDA)

The PDA prohibits discrimination on the basis of pregnancy, childbirth or related medical conditions. Women affected by pregnancy or related conditions must be treated in the same manner as other applicants or employees with similar abilities or limitations.

http://www.eeoc.gov/abouteeoc/35th/thelaw/pregnancy_discrimination-1978.html

Rehabilitation Act of 1973

Section 503 of the Rehabilitation Act requires most employers doing business with the Federal Government to take **affirmative action** to employ and advance in employment qualified individuals with a disability. Section 504 prohibits discrimination in employment against qualified individuals with a disability. A qualified individual with a disability is a person who: (1) has a physical or mental impairment which "substantially limits" one or more major life activities, (2) has a record of such impairment, or (3) is regarded as having such an impairment.

http://www.eeoc.gov/policy/rehab.html

Uniformed Services Employment and Reemployment Rights Act (USERRA)

The USERRA prohibits discrimination against persons because of their service in the Armed Forces Reserve, the National Guard, or other uniformed services. USERRA prohibits an employer from denying any benefit of employment on the basis of an individual's membership, application for membership, performance of service, application for service, or obligation for service in the uniformed services. USERRA also protects the right of veterans, reservists, National Guard members, and certain other members of the uniformed services to reclaim their civilian employment after being absent due to military service or training.

http://www.dol.gov/elaws/userra.htm
http://www.osc.gov/userra.htm

Vietnam Era Veterans' Readjustment Assistance Act

The law requires that employers with federal contracts or subcontracts of $25,000 or more provide equal opportunity and affirmative action for Vietnam era veterans, special disabled veterans, and veterans who served on active duty during a war or in a campaign or expedition for which a campaign badge has been authorized.

http://www.dol.gov/esa/regs/compliance/ofccp/fsvevraa.htm

APPENDIX D
EMPLOYMENT RECORD RETENTION

Fair Labor Standards Act (FLSA):

- Supplementary basic records (i.e., basic employment and earnings records and wage rate tables), order, shipping, and billing records, and records of additions to or deductions from wages paid, are required to be kept for **two years**.

- Payroll records, certificates, agreements, plans, notices, and sales and purchase records, are required to be kept for **three years**.

Civil Rights Act of 1964, Title VII, Age Discrimination in Employment Act (ADEA) and the Americans with Disabilities Act (ADA):

- Under the three Acts, employers with at least fifteen employees must retain applications and other personnel records relating to hires, rehires, tests used in employment, promotion, transfers, demotions, selection for training, layoff, recall, terminations of discharge, for **one year** from making the record or taking the personnel action.

- The ADEA requires the retention of the same records for **one year** for employers with twenty or more employees.

- Title VII and the ADA require that basic employee demographic data, pay rates, and weekly compensation records be retained for at least **one year** for employers with twenty or more employees.

Family and Medical Leave Act (FMLA): The FMLA requires the retention of certain records with respect to payroll and demographic information as well as information related to the individual employee's leave of absence for **three years**.

Occupational Safety and Health Act (OSHA):

- OSHA requires that records of job-related injuries and illnesses be kept for **five years**.

- In addition, records related to medical exams along with toxic substances and blood-borne pathogen exposure must be retained for **thirty years** after termination of employment.

APPENDIX E
HR WEB SITES

GENERAL
Society of Human Resource Management (SHRM)
http://www.shrm.org
National Human Resource Association
http://www.humanresources.org/
International Public Management Association for HR
http://www.ipma-hr.org/
International Association of Human Resource Management
http://www.ihrim.org/
World Federation of Personnel Management Associations
http://www.wfpma.com/
American Association School Personnel Administrators
www.aaspa.org/index.html
College and University Professional Association of HR
http://www.cupahr.org/
Workforce Management
http://www.workforce.com
AuditNet
http://www.auditnet.org
Online HR Resources
http://www.hr-guide.com/
HRM Guide
http://www.hrmguide.com/
HR Metrics
http://hrmetrics.org/MetricsCategories.aspx
SHRM Benchmarking Service
http://www.shrm.org/research/benchmarks/#1
HR Executive Online
http://www.hreonline.com/HRE/index.jsp

84 Auditing Human Resources

WORKFORCE PLANNING AND EMPLOYMENT
US Equal Employment Opportunity Commission
http://www.eeoc.gov/
US Department of Labor
http://www.dol.gov/
Organizational Design Forum
http://www.organizationdesignforum.org/
Equal Employment Opportunity Commission
http://www.eeoc.gov/
INS and I-9 Information
http://uscis.gov/graphics/index.htm
Federal Trade Commission - Fair Credit Reporting Act Information
http://www.ftc.gov
Social Security Administration - Verification of SSNs
http://www.ssa.gov

HUMAN RESOURCE DEVELOPMENT
American Society of Training and Development (ASTD)
http://www.astd.org
Academy of Human Resource Development
http://www.academyofhrd.org/

TOTAL REWARDS
World at Work (National Compensation Association)
http://www.worldatwork.org/
American Benefits Council
http://www.americanbenefitscouncil.org
DOL - Wage and Hour Regulations
http://www.dol.gov/dol/allcfr/Title_29/Chapter_V.htm

EMPLOYEE AND LABOR RELATIONS
American Arbitration Association
http://www.adr.org/
National Labor Relations Board
http://www.nlrb.gov/
Federal Labor Relations Authority
http://www.flra.gov/

RISK MANAGEMENT
Risk Management Association
http://www.rmahq.org/RMA/
Occupational Safety and Health Administration
http://www.osha.gov

APPENDIX F
SAMPLE AUDIT PROGRAM

Preliminary Steps

Objective: To ensure that proper HR controls, policies, and procedures are in place and in compliance with applicable laws and regulations.

Audit Procedure	W/P Ref	Initial/ Date	Comments/ Findings
1. Prepare and send an entrance letter to HR executive.			
2. Clearly define audit objectives and scope.			
3. Conduct an in-house review of the following: a. Internal policy and procedures manuals			
b. Applicable rules, laws, and regulations			
c. Management data reports			
d. Prior internal audit reports and management comments			
e. HR self-assessment reports			

Audit Procedure	W/P Ref	Initial/ Date	Comments/ Findings
4. Schedule and hold an entrance conference with the HR department key staff. Obtain the name of the departmental contact person and secure a place from which to conduct the fieldwork portion of the audit.			
5. Survey (by e-mail) key users (management staff). Conduct interviews of HR staff and other key users. Document the interviews in the audit file.			
6. Prepare an initial information request to include the following: a. Organizational strategic plan			
b. HR strategic and operational plans			
c. High-level organizational chart (showing HR department relationship within overall structure)			
d. HR department organizational chart			
e. HR customer surveys			
f. HR performance assessment tools			

Audit Procedure	W/P Ref	Initial/ Date	Comments/ Findings
g. HR staff experience and education summary			
h. Workforce plans			
i. Recruitment and selection policies and procedures			
j. Employee turnover reports			
k. Employee exit surveys			
l. Training plans and course schedules			
m. Management training course schedule			
n. New employee orientation summary			
o. Compensation and benefit policies and procedures			
p. FLSA status listing by job title			
q. EEO reports			
r. Employee Handbook (policies and procedures)			
s. Employee performance appraisal form examples			
7. Conduct HR budget review to determine whether expenses are reasonable, properly recorded, and that adequate controls exist.			

Audit Procedure	W/P Ref	Initial/ Date	Comments/ Findings
8. After gaining an understanding of various functions, conduct preliminary risk assessment.			
9. Prepare a risk assessment summary of the strengths and weaknesses of the HR program. Discuss the areas of greatest risk and exposure. Also, include suggested audit objectives and test procedures. Discuss with audit supervisor.			
10. Prepare the audit program and include a time budget and estimated completion date.			
11. Clear review notes and revise the audit program, if necessary.			

General HR Department Review

Objective: To determine whether HR department is viewed as a strategic business partner, a trusted advisor to management, helpful and accessible to employees, protecting organizational risk but allowing management to make quick important decisions, and a provider of accurate data.

Audit Procedure	W/P Ref	Initial/ Date	Comments/ Findings
1. Review organizational strategic plan and HR strategic plan. Test to ensure that HR has long-term strategic plan that links to overall workforce objectives for the organization.			
2. Review HR operational plan. Test to ensure that HR has set key result areas for the department, task/project plans have been developed, tasks have been assigned internally, and decisions to use outside vendors are adequately supported.			

Audit Procedure	W/P Ref	Initial/ Date	Comments/ Findings
3. Review HR performance assessment methods. Test to ensure that annual performance assessments are conducted, appropriate and approved performance standards have been established, and ongoing HR metrics are measured against benchmarking standards.			
4. Review HR department organizational chart, HR staff job descriptions, and HR department employee turnover rate. Determine whether senior HR management position is at an appropriate level within the organization to provide strategic HR services. Determine whether HR staff is appropriately utilized to provide services laid out in HR operational plan.			

Audit Procedure	W/P Ref	Initial/ Date	Comments/ Findings
5. Review HR staff competencies and continuing education. Determine whether HR staff have appropriate education, experience and training to perform duties assigned. Test to determine whether HR staff attends appropriate levels of continuing education to be knowledgeable regarding professional standards and employment regulations.			
6. Conduct a site walk-through to determine if there are any clear issues with HR department facilities (e.g., job candidate reception area, appropriate employment notices posted, private area for interviews and employee/ manager consultations).			

94 Auditing Human Resources

Audit Procedure	W/P Ref	Initial/ Date	Comments/ Findings
7. Review HR automated systems. Test to determine whether technology up-to-date in order to provide accurate and timely service. Verify that appropriate backup and recovery procedures exist for HRIS. Test system security to make certain that employees have appropriate access to different levels of data.			
8. Review HR information management processes. Review a sample of management reports, tracing data to source system to verify accuracy of information. Determine if any reports are being created that are not being reviewed and/or are unnecessary.			

Workforce Planning and Employment

Objective: To determine whether appropriate workforce levels are met, employees are recruited and selected to create a diverse workforce, that contract workforce is appropriately managed, and that organization is in compliance with all employment regulations.

Audit Procedure	W/P Ref	Initial/ Date	Comments/ Findings
1. Review workforce plan documents to determine whether: a. The workforce plan is linked to the organization's strategic mission.			
b. Current and future workforce profiles are developed and gap analysis is performed. Are there any critical skills shortages?			
c. Workforce demographics reveal any unusual data trends.			
d. HR has performed environmental scans to determine impact on workforce.			
e. HR has forecast the number and specified positions that need to be filled.			

Audit Procedure	W/P Ref	Initial/ Date	Comments/ Findings
f. The projected staff requirements are used in planning recruitment activities and training and development programs to be offered.			
2. Review a sample of job vacancies to determine they are developed from a current position description or recent job analysis.			
3. Obtain recruitment action plans to determine whether they include budgets and timelines for addressing job vacancies and/or new positions.			
4. Review EEO/Diversity plan regarding recruitment goals. Test EEO trends to determine whether progress is being made towards diversity goals.			

Audit Procedure	W/P Ref	Initial/ Date	Comments/ Findings
5. Determine whether recruitment sources are periodically evaluated to ensure that they are meeting the needs of the organization (may need to review recruiting metrics such as time-to-fill or cost-per-hire).			
6. Determine whether any applicants tests (e.g., typing, psychological/personality, cognitive, assessment center, motor/physical assessment) or standardized scoring tools (e.g., selection matrix) are reviewed by HR to ensure their reliability and validity?			
7. Determine whether employees who interview candidates have been trained in the types of questions and actions that are legal to ask in hiring process.			

Audit Procedure	W/P Ref	Initial/ Date	Comments/ Findings
8. Test sample of employment documents to ensure they are available, accurate, and complete. (This includes applications, resumes, test results, interview questions, recruiting summary, reasons for hiring versus not hiring, and so forth.)			
9. Test a sample of recently hired employees to ensure that: a. Background checks are conducted on all applicants to verify information reported in application (e.g., prior employment history, education, certification/ license).			
b. Reference checks were conducted before offer was made.			

Audit Procedure	W/P Ref	Initial/ Date	Comments/ Findings
c. Criminal background checks were conducted on all applicants for positions of a sensitive nature (e.g., handle money; direct contact with children, elderly or disabled, access to controlled substances) and that the results were received before final offer was made.			
10. Determine whether any required applicant drug tests are conducted if appropriate for the position (e.g., truck drivers, medical staff). Test a sample of records to determine whether: a. Drug testing policy is consistently applied.			
b. Drug tests are performed and results are received before final offer is made.			

100 Auditing Human Resources

Audit Procedure	W/P Ref	Initial/ Date	Comments/ Findings
11. Review independent contractor policies and procedures and a sample of independent contractor contracts to ensure appropriate management controls exist and that IRS rules are met.			
12. Review the process for terminating employees. Determine whether exit interviews or exit surveys are conducted with all employees who are voluntarily terminated. Determine whether HR computes employee turnover rate, reasons for turnover and related replacement costs. Select a sample of terminated employees and obtain evidence that appropriate procedures were followed and that the legal department was involved. Test a sample of terminated employee files to ensure that COBRA notifications sent to terminated employees within two weeks after notification of termination.			

Audit Procedure	W/P Ref	Initial/ Date	Comments/ Findings
13. Review the process for terminating employees. Determine whether exit interviews or exit surveys are conducted with all employees who are voluntarily terminated. Determine whether HR computes employee turnover rate, reasons for turnover and related replacement costs. Select a sample of terminated employees and obtain evidence that appropriate procedures were followed and that the legal department was involved. Test a sample of terminated employee files to ensure that COBRA notifications sent to terminated employees within two weeks after notification of termination.			
14. Review hiring policies and procedures to determine whether: a. Recruitment and selection processes are supported by written policies and procedures that are updated, accurate, and complete.			

Audit Procedure	W/P Ref	Initial/ Date	Comments/ Findings
b. Managers and interviewers are provided resources regarding recruitment and selection laws and regulations.			
c. Federal EEO reports are submitted as required (see www.eeoc.gov/employers/ surveys.html).			
d. Applicant data for those not hired are retained for two years.			
e. Hiring area has a bulletin board with all legally required notices on display.			
15. Determine whether employees receive fraud training and sign that they have received a copy of the organization's fraud policy and code of ethics.			
16. Ensure that an anonymous fraud reporting system exists and that the system is promoted to employees.			

Human Resource Development

Objective: To determine whether appropriate levels of training are provided to ensure employees have the necessary skills.

Audit Procedure	W/P Ref	Initial/ Date	Comments/ Findings
1. Test a sample of new employee records to determine whether employees attended new employee orientation within first 30 days of employment.			
2. Review new employee orientation outline to determine whether the following issues are covered: a. Insurance and benefits information			
b. Grievance policy			
c. Disciplinary action policy			
d. Safety and security issues			
e. Worker's compensation			
f. Performance appraisal process			
g. Sexual harassment issues			
h. Employee leave policies			
i. Americans with Disabilities Act			

Audit Procedure	W/P Ref	Initial/ Date	Comments/ Findings
j. Equal Employment Opportunity related topics			
k. Privacy, information security, and technology			
3. Review technical training program(s) to determine whether: a. Skill-based training programs are available for skills sets unique to the organization.			
b. Training programs have clearly established and specific behavioral objectives.			
c. Employees who deliver training or outside trainers are required to be knowledgeable in the contents of the programs they deliver.			
d. Employees who deliver training have received train-the-trainer instruction.			

Audit Procedure	W/P Ref	Initial/ Date	Comments/ Findings
4. Test a sample of employee records to determine whether new managerial employees have attended management training within first 90 days after promotion/hire.			
5. Review supervisory training course outline schedule to determine whether the following issues are covered: a. Basic management principals			
b. Employment law			
c. How to deal with employee issues			
d. Employee performance management			
6. Review organization's process for assessing the value of training programs to determine whether results of training programs are continually monitored and evaluated.			

106 Auditing Human Resources

Audit Procedure	W/P Ref	Initial/ Date	Comments/ Findings
7. Obtain copy of all performance appraisal forms used. Review appraisal forms to determine whether appraisals are based on specific job-related criteria rather than employee behaviors or personal traits.			
8. Review sample of completed performance appraisals to determine if form was completed within time stated by policy (usually annually); employee has signed form indicating the form was discussed with them; supervisor comments are job-specific and appropriate. Generally, supervisor comments should not refer to an employee's medical issues or time away from work if granted to comply with state or federal law (family and medical leave, leave associated with a disability, worker's compensation leave).			

Audit Procedure	W/P Ref	Initial/ Date	Comments/ Findings
9. Review performance improvement/counseling policy and procedures. Verify that HR tracks all employees on formal performance improvement plans and monitors deadlines with supervisor.			
10. Review sample of documentation regarding employees in performance improvement plans to ensure appropriate support, action plan, employee acknowledgement and final settlement is documented.			
11. Determine whether an external employee assistance program (EAP) is available for employees. Review how employees are notified of EAP services and how to contact the provider.			

Audit Procedure	W/P Ref	Initial/ Date	Comments/ Findings
12. Review disciplinary action policy and procedures. Obtain list from HR of all employee disciplinary actions taken. Test sample of disciplinary actions to ensure proper support, action steps, and employee acknowledgement are documented. Determine if disciplinary actions appear consistent for similar problems across the organization.			

Total Rewards

Objective: To determine whether compensation and benefit programs provide adequate pay to recruit and retain a talented workforce and to comply with applicable regulations.

Audit Procedure	W/P Ref	Initial/ Date	Comments/ Findings
1. Review sample of current job descriptions to ensure that essential job duties; knowledge, skills, abilities; education, and experience are appropriate for job. Ensure that job descriptions do not have physical requirements that are not essential to the job (Americans with Disabilities Act violation).			
2. Review procedure for analysis of position salaries compared to the market. Review internal or external vendor reports regarding analysis of compensation surveys and organizational policy on revising salaries.			

Audit Procedure	W/P Ref	Initial/ Date	Comments/ Findings
3. Review process of how HR decides how to place positions into appropriate job title and salary level. Review sample of job audits for thorough review and consistent criteria for making salary grade slotting determinations.			
4. Determine whether HR has process to review positions to ensure internal salary equity of positions across the organization.			
5. Determine whether there is a process for employees to request a review of their position if they believe they are misclassified in an incorrect title or level.			
6. Determine whether HR staff or contracted vendor has appropriate compensation expertise to perform job evaluation analysis.			

Audit Procedure	W/P Ref	Initial/ Date	Comments/ Findings
7. Review salary administration procedures. a. Determine whether specific guidelines are provided to supervisors for salary adjustments.			
b. Test sample of employee promotions and pay for performance increases to determine whether they are appropriately supported by documented justification.			
c. Determine whether executive compensation programs are appropriately administered (e.g., stock purchase, stock options, incentive, bonus, supplemental retirement plan).			
d. Determine whether expatriate and foreign national reward systems are appropriately administered.			
e. Determine whether HR reviews salary actions to ensure they are nondiscriminatory.			

Audit Procedure	W/P Ref	Initial/ Date	Comments/ Findings
8. Test a sample of FLSA determinations for compliance with regulations.			
9. Test a sample of timesheets for appropriate overtime calculations.			
10. Review employee benefits program to ensure: a. Benefit program applies to all employees. b. Benefits information is communicated to employees. c. Process for filing claims, challenging benefits determinations, and changing coverage is adequate.			
11. Review paid leave policies and procedures. a. Test sample of paid leave calculations to ensure procedures are followed consistently.			

Audit Procedure	W/P Ref	Initial/ Date	Comments/ Findings
b. Review the files and paperwork for those individuals who have taken leave under the Family Medical Leave Act. Determine if proper notifications were made, that the leave was properly administered, that the company makes contact with the employee on leave, and in other ways comply with the law.			
12. Review retirement plan to ensure that: a. All employees are allowed to participate.			
b. The vesting period is the same for all employees.			
13. Review HR process for communicating payroll information (e.g., new hires, deductions, adjustments, terminations) to payroll department.			

Audit Procedure	W/P Ref	Initial/ Date	Comments/ Findings
14. Test to ensure that payroll master file has accurate employee data.			
15. Review to ensure appropriate controls are in place to approve payroll file changes.			
16. Test to determine whether access to payroll file data is restricted to authorized staff. And automated payroll data is safeguarded with appropriate security controls.			
17. Review monthly reconciliations between payroll file and accounting records.			
18. Determine whether preliminary payroll report is checked against previous month to detect any significant deviations.			
19. Assess whether payroll file is monthly reconciled against tax reporting.			

Audit Procedure	W/P Ref	Initial/ Date	Comments/ Findings
20. Test a sample of records to ensure employees have accurate payroll deduction calculations.			
21. Review to determine whether supplemental payrolls are not used to regularly process regular payroll mistakes or oversights.			

Employee and Labor Relations

Objective: To determine whether organization is in compliance with employment regulations and that employee complaints and grievance are handled appropriately.

Audit Procedure	W/P Ref	Initial/ Date	Comments/ Findings
1. Obtain Employee Handbook. Review policies and procedures to ensure appropriate coverage and that they are in compliance with federal and state regulations and consistently applied. Handbook should: a. Not create a contract, express or implied.			

Audit Procedure	W/P Ref	Initial/ Date	Comments/ Findings
b. Include a statement that the handbook is not all-inclusive, and is only a set of guidelines.			
c. Does not alter the "at-will" relationship between employer and employee.			
d. Not guarantee employment for any definite period of time.			
e. Apply to all employees, and that no category of employees is excluded.			
f. State that the handbook can be changed by the organization unilaterally, at any time.			
2. Obtain recent employee attitude surveys and reports. Determine whether management has procedures in place to take action on issues raised in the survey.			

Audit Procedure	W/P Ref	Initial/ Date	Comments/ Findings
3. Conduct site check to ensure that all employee records/ personnel files are kept in a secured location with controlled access and that they are kept in an environmentally safe location (i.e., fire/water/ insect proof).			
4. Conduct test of a sample of personnel files to ensure that files: a. Include complete and appropriate information.			
b. Employee medical information, including family and medical leave and disability accommodation requests, is kept in files separate from general personnel file.			
c. All Employment Eligibility Verification (I-9) forms and any other documentation identifying EEO data are kept separate from general personnel file.			

Audit Procedure	W/P Ref	Initial/ Date	Comments/ Findings
5. Conduct test of a sample of I-9 forms to ensure appropriate documentation is provided and submitted within three days of hire.			
6. Determine whether employee records are retained for four years.			
7. Review HR files to determine whether procedures are in place for the identification, documentation, investigation, and final resolution of employee grievances. Test a sample of employee grievance files to ensure that appropriate documentation and resolution is provided.			
8. Determine whether HR has controls in place to ensure that they are aware of all employee complaints.			
9. Conduct site review to ensure that all employee complaints and grievances and related documentation are filed in a secure location.			

Audit Procedure	W/P Ref	Initial/ Date	Comments/ Findings
10. Determine whether HR analyzes the causes of complaints and grievances and makes recommendations for corrective and preventive measures to reduce the number of complaints and grievances filed.			
11. Determine if there is any outstanding employment litigation. Review trends in the number and reasons for employee lawsuits against organization.			
12. Observe that the required employment postings are posted in a location viewable by all employees.			
13. Determine if there are any employees utilizing the Americans with Disabilities Act (ADA) accommodation and test the approval process for compliance with the law.			

Risk Management

Objective: To determine whether employee safety programs are implemented and workers compensation is in compliance with applicable regulations.

Audit Procedure	W/P Ref	Initial/ Date	Comments/ Findings
1. Review accident reports, showing documentation of personal injury and property damage. Compare trend data to industry reports for any issues.			
2. Review worker's compensation data reports.			

HR Services Outsourcing and Co-sourcing

Objective: To determine whether outsourced HR programs are appropriately awarded and managed.

Audit Procedure	W/P Ref	Initial/ Date	Comments/ Findings
1. Review the selection process for HR outsourcing/co-sourcing vendor(s) and periodic fee negotiations. Test current contracts and amendments to determine if clear selection criteria were used to make awards that appropriate performance standards are set in the contract, that sufficient service level agreements and guarantees/incentives are included in contract.			
2. Review any internal reviews conducted of vendor performance.			
3. Conduct a test of a sample of vendor fees for appropriateness.			

Audit Wrap-up			
Audit Procedure	W/P Ref	Initial/ Date	Comments/ Findings
1. Summarize potential audit findings.			
2. Discuss any audit findings with the audit supervisor.			
3. Complete and index working papers.			
4. Prepare a preliminary draft of the audit report.			
5. Clear review notes.			
6. Hold status meetings with client and discuss draft audit report.			
7. Incorporate client responses into the final audit report.			
8. If requested, schedule and hold exit conference.			
9. Present the audit report.			

APPENDIX G
REFERENCES

[1] Kimberly A. Mock, SPHR, "Human Resource Risk Management," Society for Human Resource Management, January 2004, Retrieved May 14, 2007
http://www.shrm.org/hrresources/whitepapers_published/CMS_007222.asp

[2] "SHRM HR Glossary of Terms," Society for Human Resource Management, Retrieved May 17, 2007, <www.shrm.org/hrresources/hrglossary_published/a.asp>

[3] Mock.

[4] Nancy R. Lockwood, SPHR, GPHR, "Strategic HR Leadership – SHRM Leadership Series Part III," Society for Human Resource Management, November 2005, Retrieved April 25, 2007, <http://www.shrm.org/research/briefly_published/Leadership%20Series%20Part%20III_%20Strategic%20HR%20Leadership.asp>

[5] Rebecca R. Hastings, SPHR, "Developing an HR Budget," Society for Human Resource Management, April 2006, Retrieved May 10, 2007, <http://www.shrm.org/hrresources/whitepapers_published/CMS_016622.asp>

[6] Ibid.

[7] "HR Body of Knowledge – Strategic Management," Human Resource Certification Institute, Retrieved May 23, 2007, <http://www.hrci.org/Certification/2007HB/APX-A/>

[8] "2007 Human Resource Competency Study," Society for Human Resource Management.

[9] David Ulrich, qtd. in Kathy Gurchiek, "Credible Activism is Key HR Skill, Study Concludes," Society for Human Resource Management, 26 April 2007, Retrieved May 12, 2007, <http://www.shrm.org/hrnews_published/archives/CMS_021378.asp>

[10] Bill Leonard, "Wanted: HR Technologists," Society for Human Resource Management, December 2006, Retrieved May 14, 2006, <http://www.shrm.org/hrtx/library_published/nonIC/CMS_019709.asp>

[11] Carter McNamara, MBA, PhD, Field Guide to Consulting and Organizational Development — A Collaborative and Systems Approach to Performance, Change and Learning (Minneapolis, MN: Authenticity Consulting, 2006).

[12] David Wylie, "HR stands as first line of defense for fraud," *Austin Business Journal*, August 2002, Retrieved July 12, 2007, <http://www.bizjournals.com/austin/stories/2002/08/12/focus4.html>

[13] "Eight Tips to Preventing Employee Theft and Fraud," *All Business*, Retrieved July 12, 2007, <http://www.allbusiness.com/human-resources/workplace-health-safety-security/3935-1.html>

[14] Ibid.

[15] Ibid.

[16] W. Edwards Deming, *Out of Crisis* (Cambridge, MA: MIT Press, 1982).

[17] Stephen Grimaldi, "A Quick Breakdown of Competitive Pay," *Workforce*, December 1999, Vol. 78, No. 12, pp. 72-75.

[18] Don Espersen, "Auditing Your HR Function: Complex HR Activities," (Altamonte Springs, FL: The Institute of Internal Auditors, 2007).

[19] Garry Ritzky, SPHR, "Basic Risk Management for the HR Professional," Society for Human Resource Management, December 1997, Retrieved May 20, 2007. <http://www.shrm.org/hrresources/whitepapers_published/CMS_000247.asp>

[20] "What is a Safety and Health Program?," Occupational Safety and Health Administration, Retrieved May 20, 2007, <http://www.osha.gov/SLTC/safetyhealth/recognition.html>

[21] Ritzky.

[22] "Survey Highlights – Outsourcing: Trends & Insights 2005," Hewitt Associates, Retrieved April 26, 2007, <http://www.hewittassociates.com/_MetaBasicCMAssetCache_/Assets/Articles/hrtrends_highlights.pdf>

[23]Ibid.
[24]"State of Texas Contract Management Guide," Texas Building and Procurement Commission, 1 March 2007, Retrieved 22 May, 2007, <http://www.tbpc.state.tx.us/communities/procurement/pub/contractguide>